SCHMITT

Op. 16

Preparatory Exercises for the Piano

Includes SCALE APPENDIX by L. Kohler

ISBN 979-8-3501-4341-6

WILLIS MUSIC

Exclusively Distributed By

HAL•LEONARD®

A Muse Group Company

Visit Hal Leonard Online at
www.halleonard.com

World headquarters, contact:
Hal Leonard
7777 West Bluemound Road
Milwaukee, WI 53213
Email: info@halleonard.com

In Europe, contact:
Hal Leonard Europe Limited
Dettingen Way
Bury St Edmunds, Suffolk, IP33 3YB
Email: info@halleonardeurope.com

In Australia, contact:
Hal Leonard Australia Pty. Ltd.
4 Lentara Court
Cheltenham, Victoria, 3192 Australia
Email: info@halleonard.com.au

Preparatory Exercises.

Specially edited and revised with Preparatory exercises for Scales and Arpeggios.

ALOYS SCHMITT.

9
10
11
12
13
14
15
16
17
18

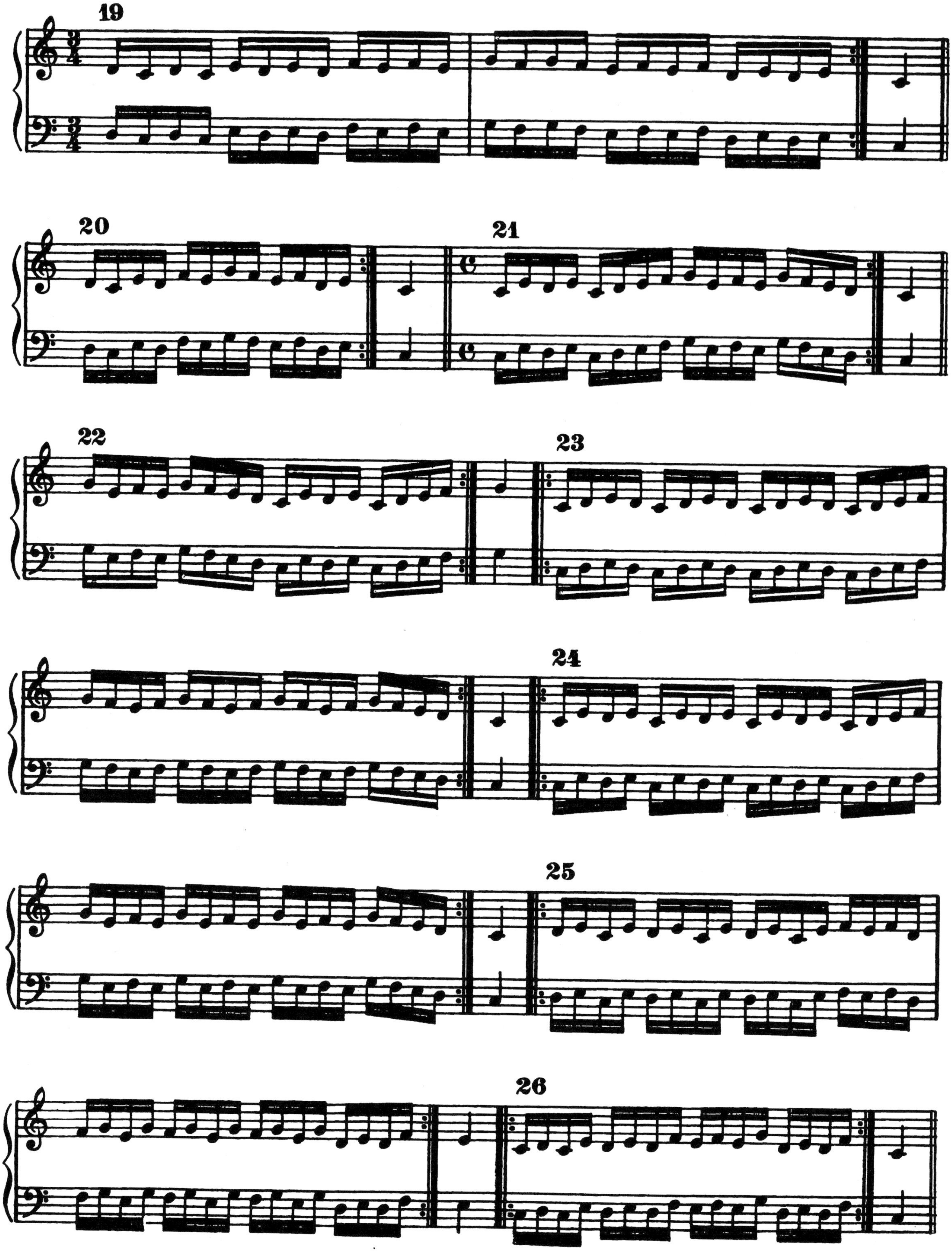
19
20
21
22
23
24
25
26

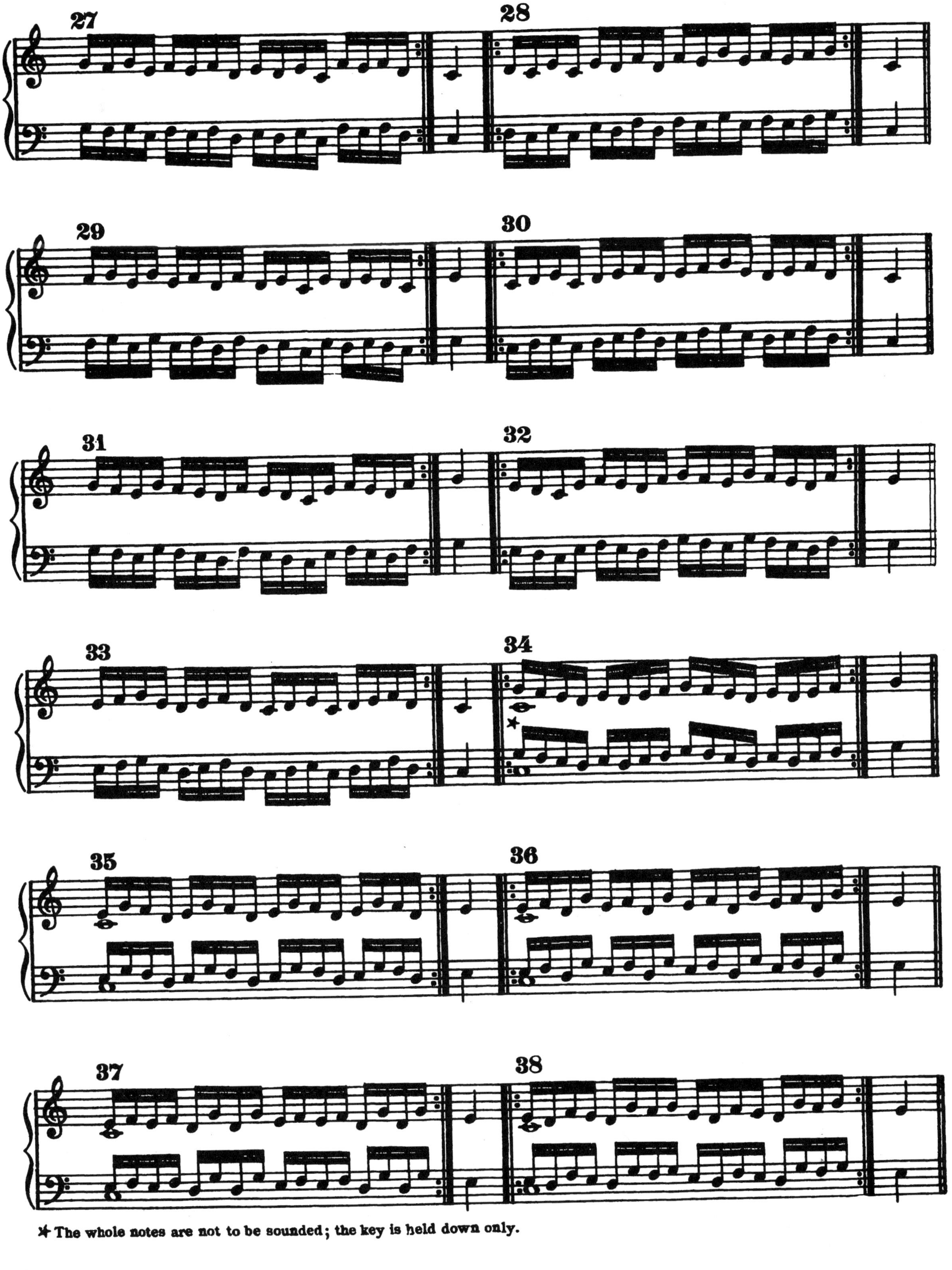

✱ The whole notes are not to be sounded; the key is held down only.

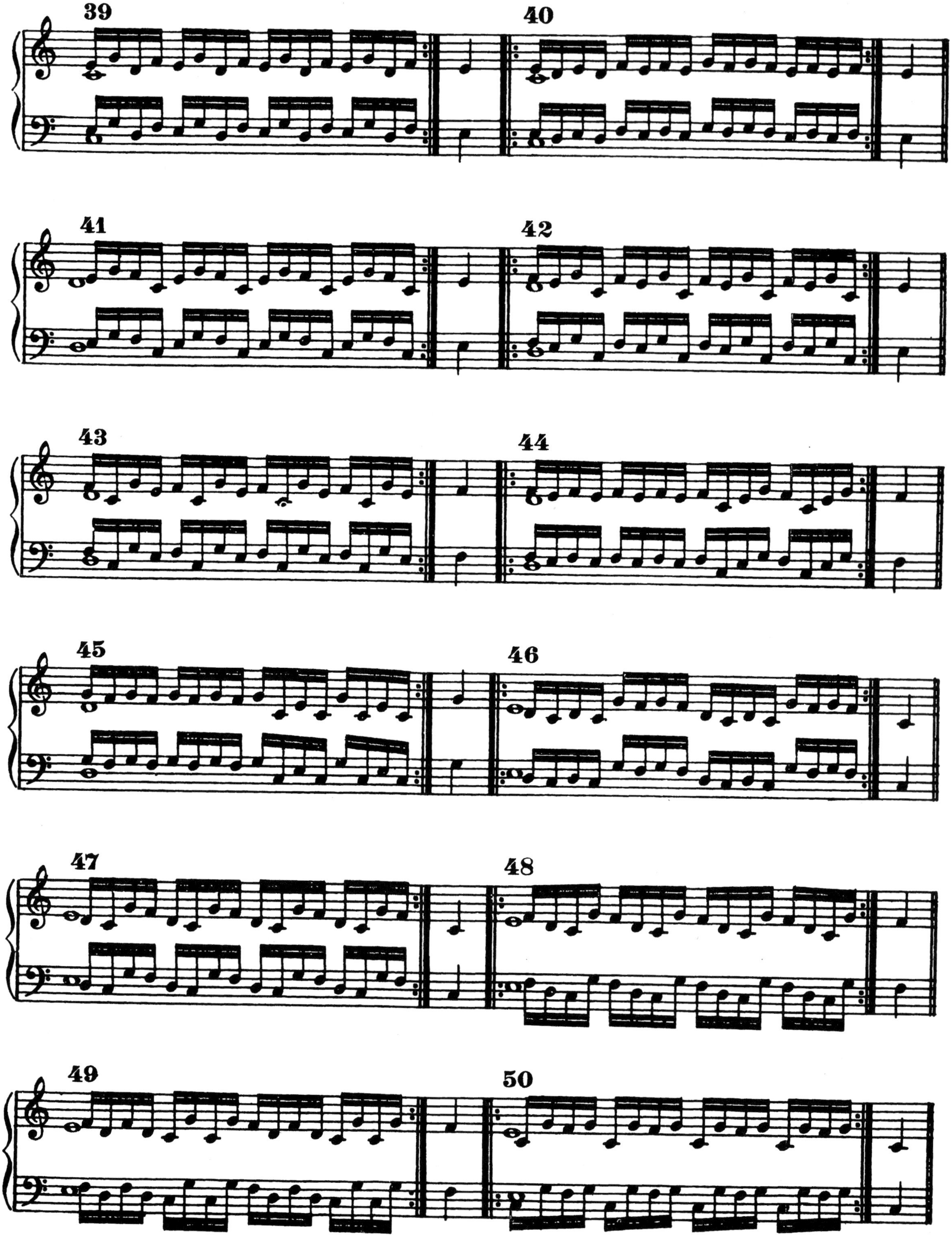
39
40
41
42
43
44
45
46
47
48
49
50

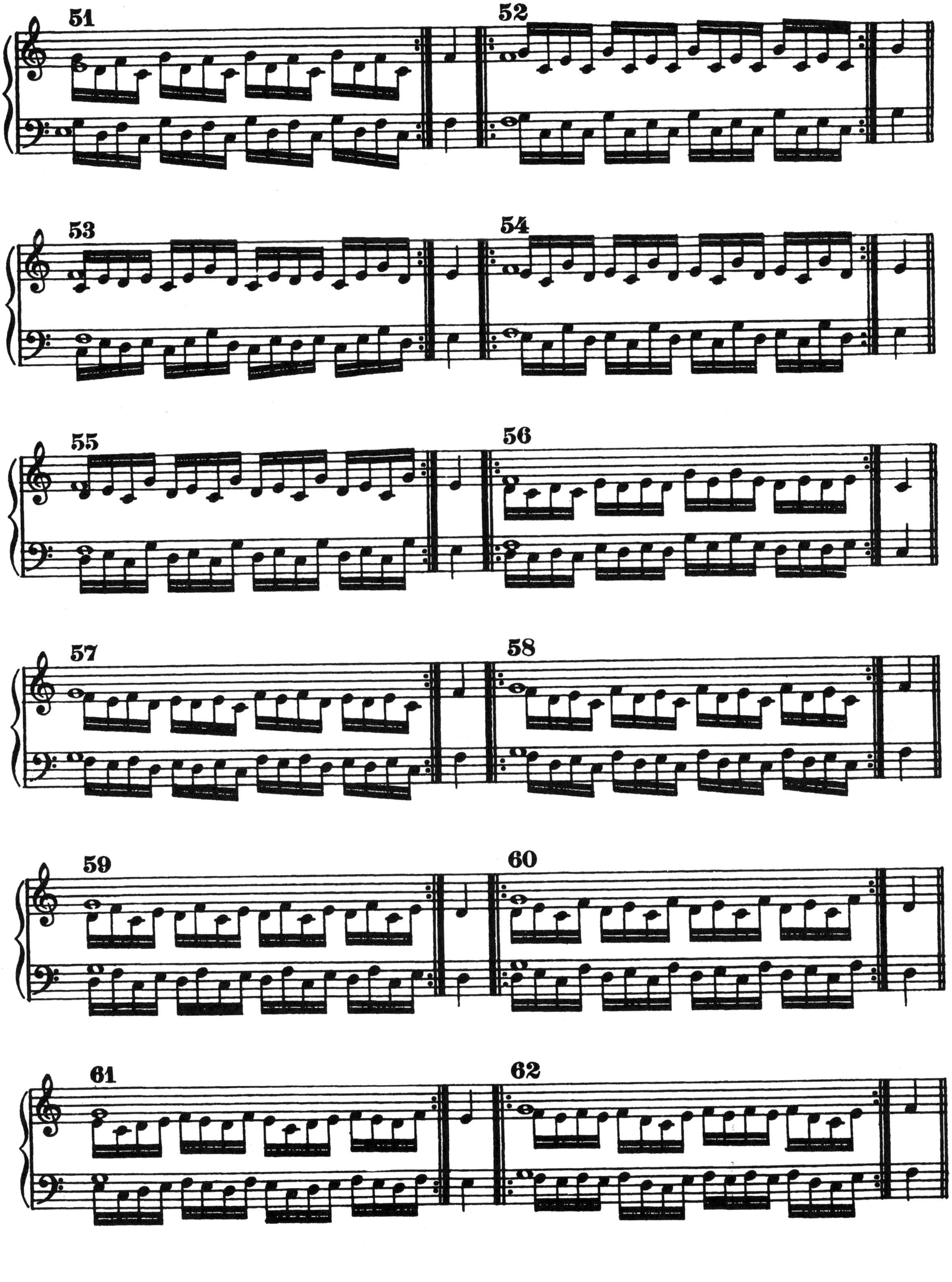
51
52
53
54
55
56
57
58
59
60
61
62

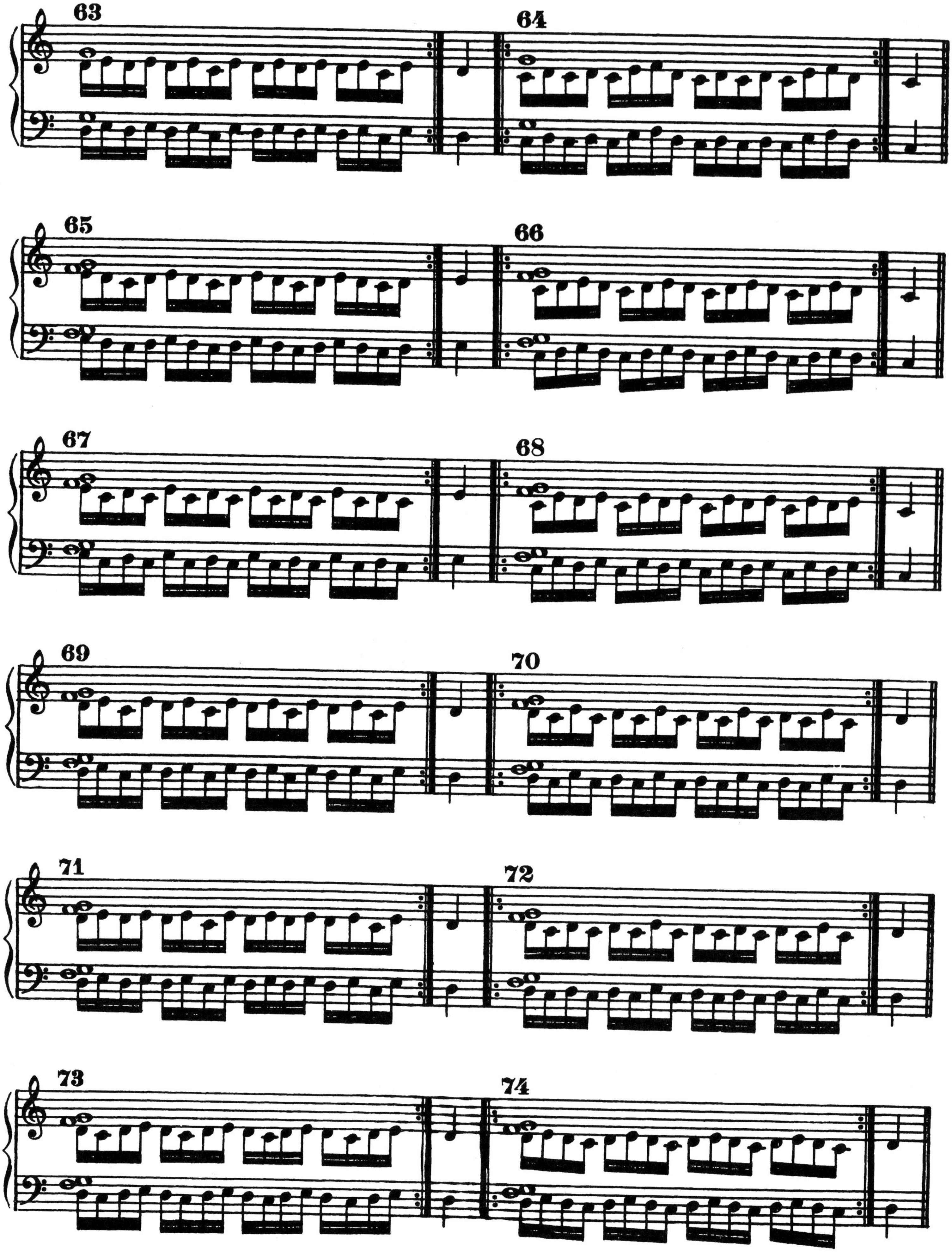
63
64
65
66
67
68
69
70
71
72
73
74

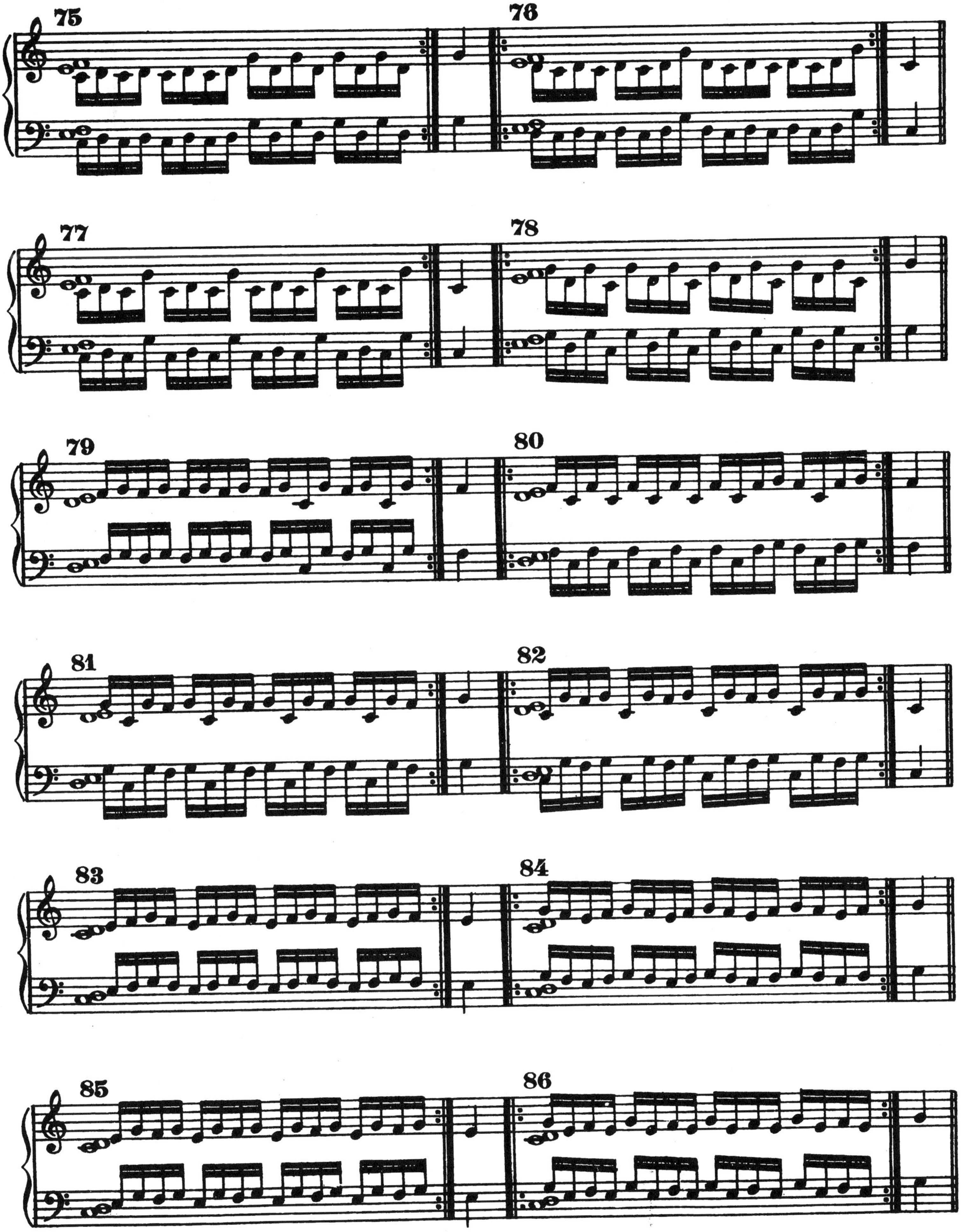
75
76
77
78
79
80
81
82
83
84
85
86

87
88
89
90
91
92
93
94
95
96
97
98

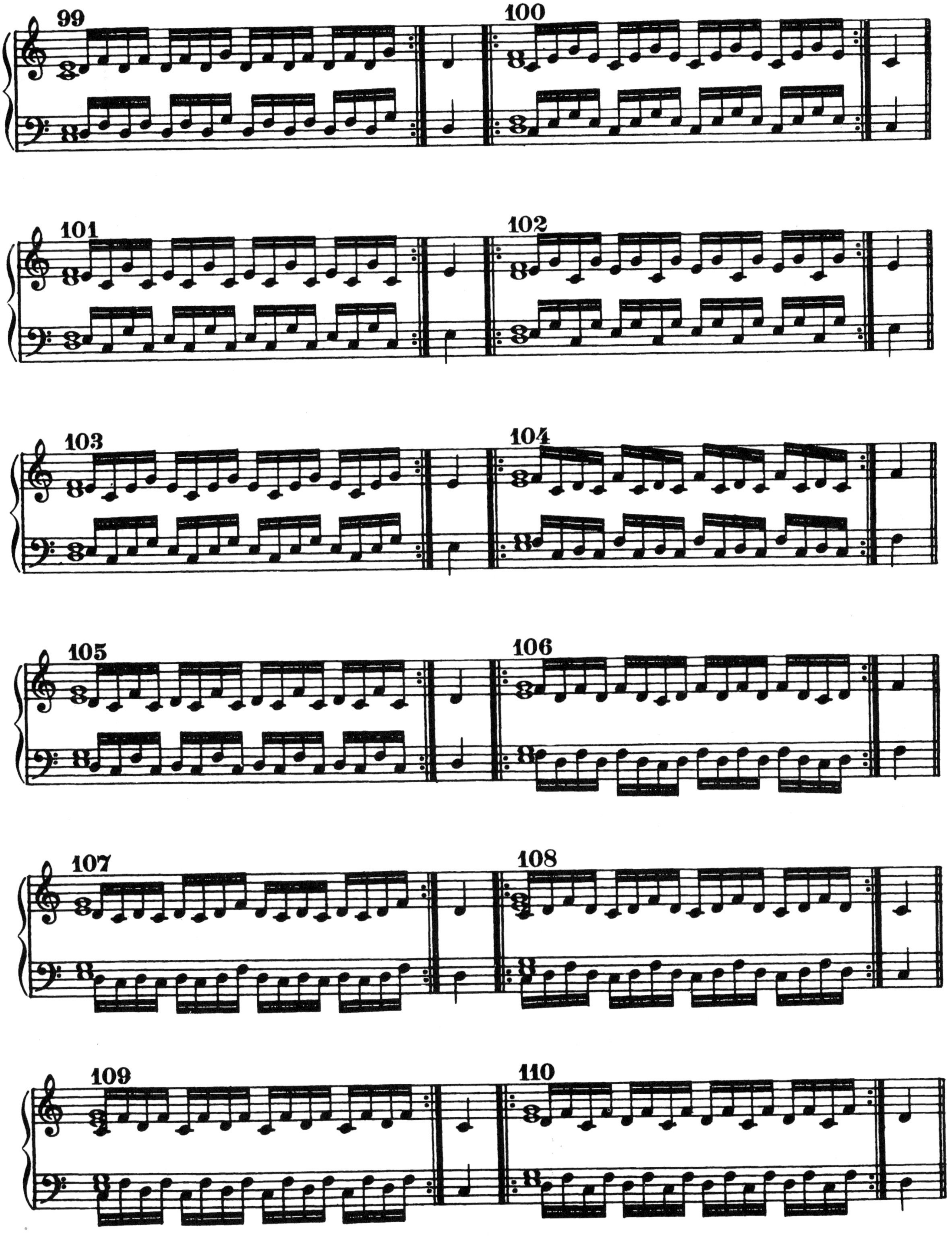
99
100
101
102
103
104
105
106
107
108
109
110

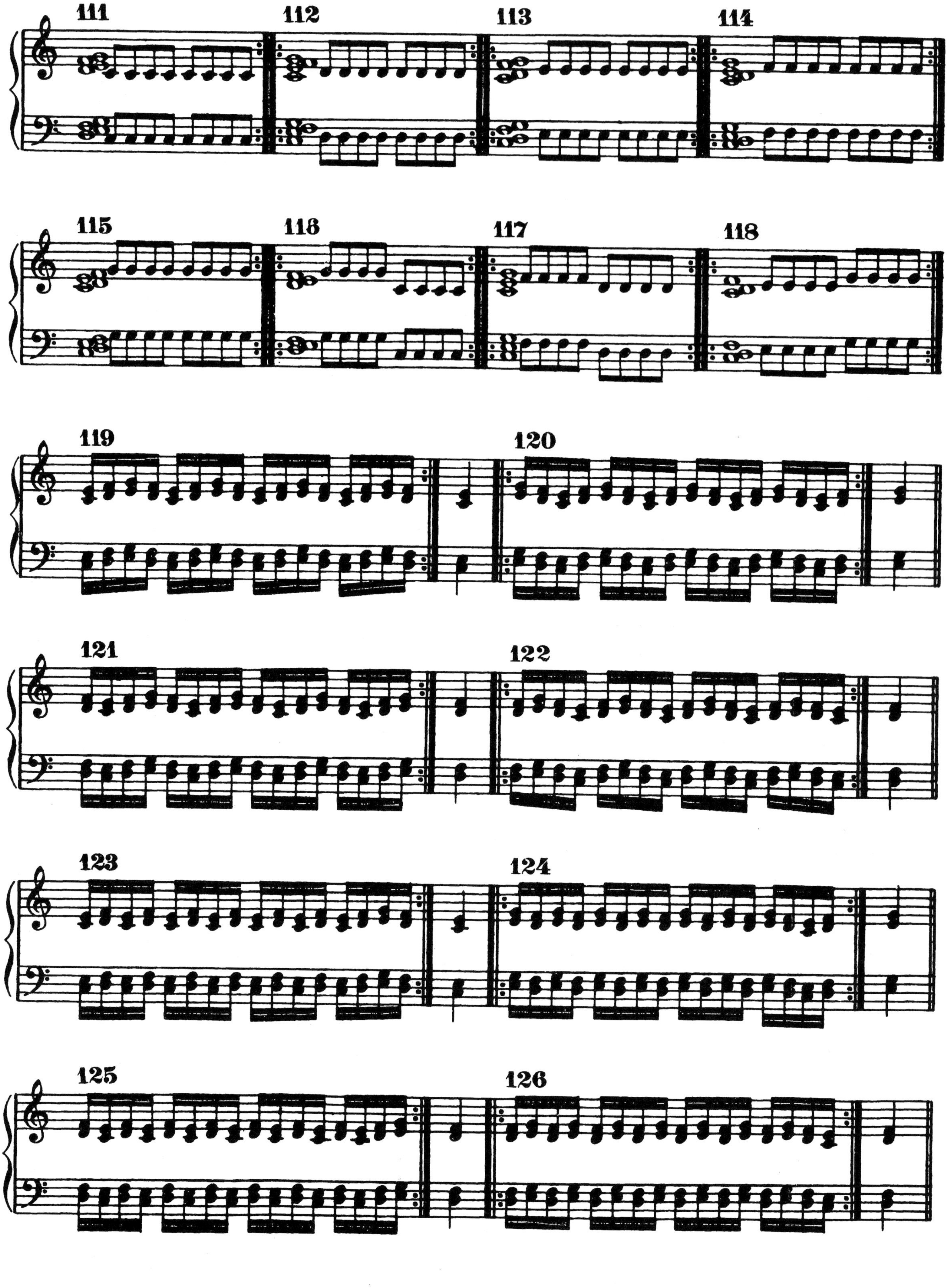
111
112
113
114
115
116
117
118
119
120
121
122
123
124
125
126

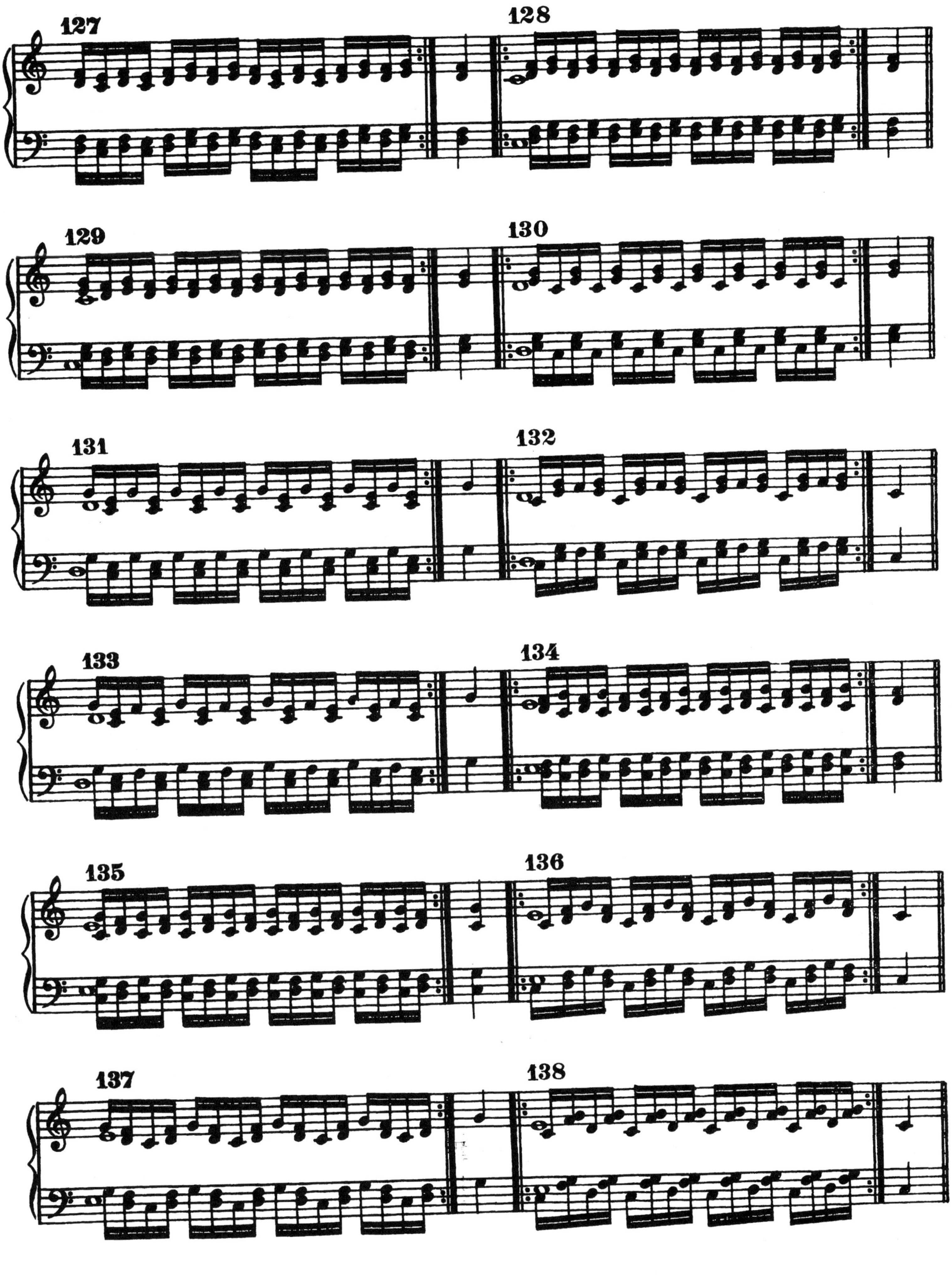
127
128
129
130
131
132
133
134
135
136
137
138

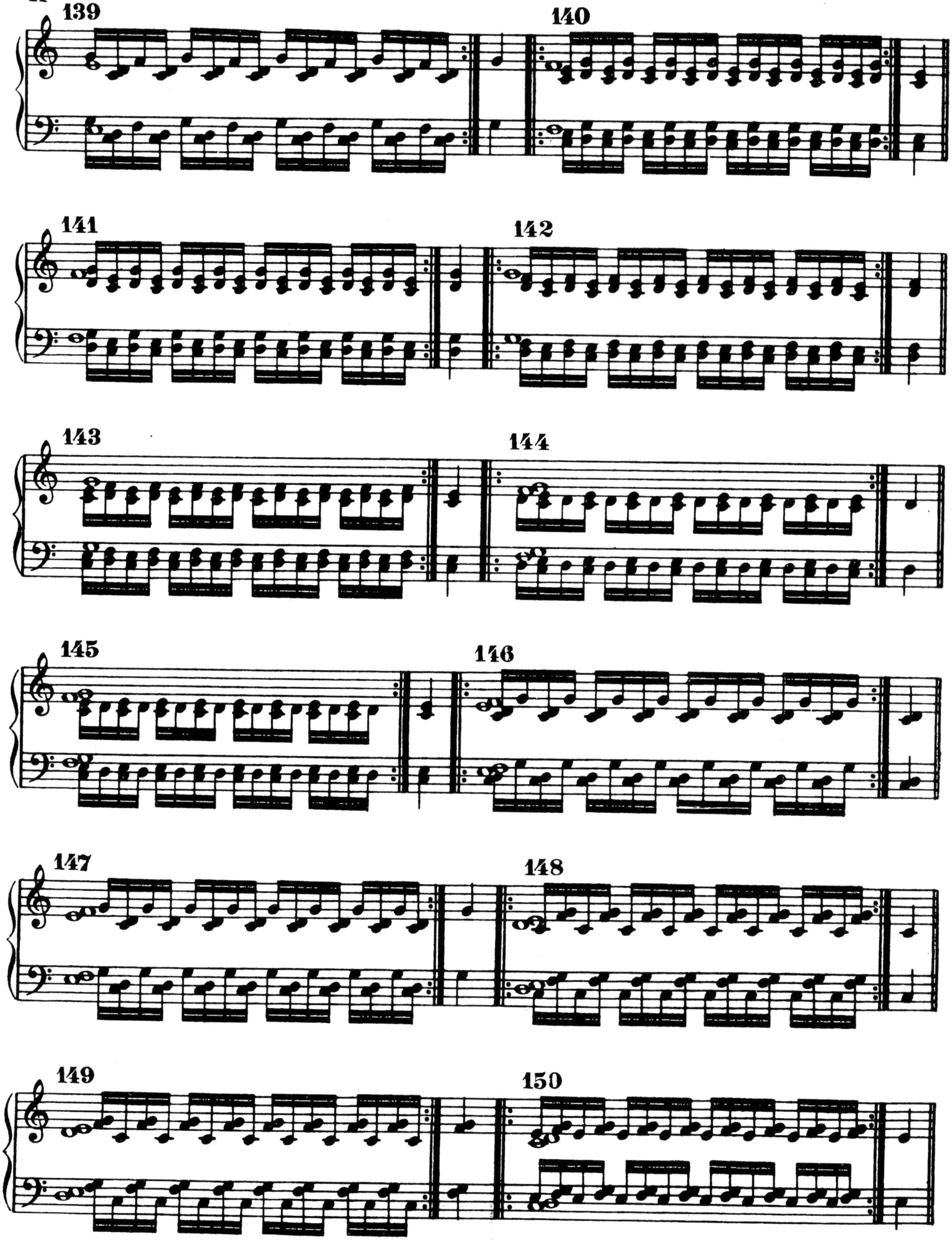
139
140
141
142
143
144
145
146
147
148
149
150

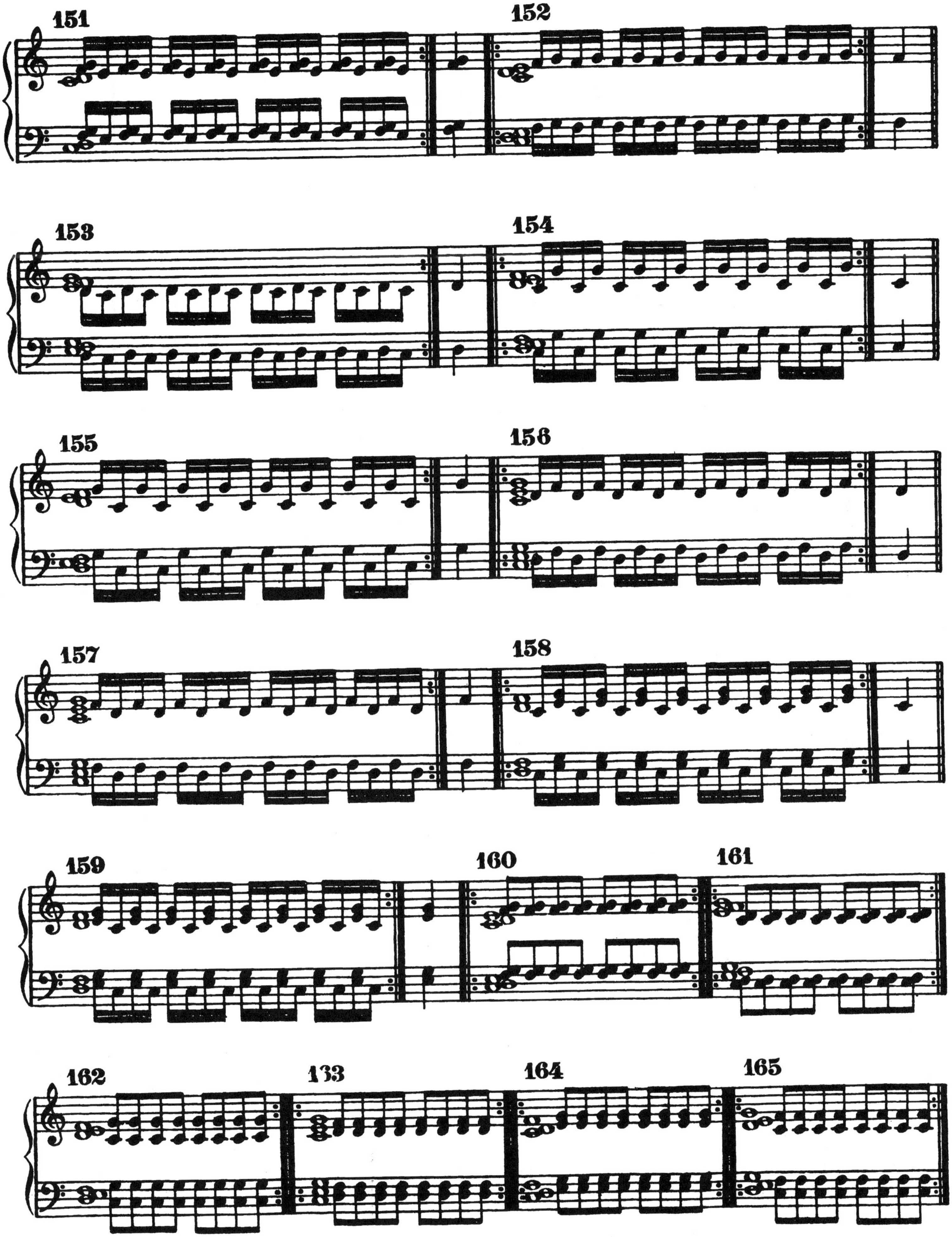
151
152
153
154
155
156
157
158
159
160
161
162
133
164
165

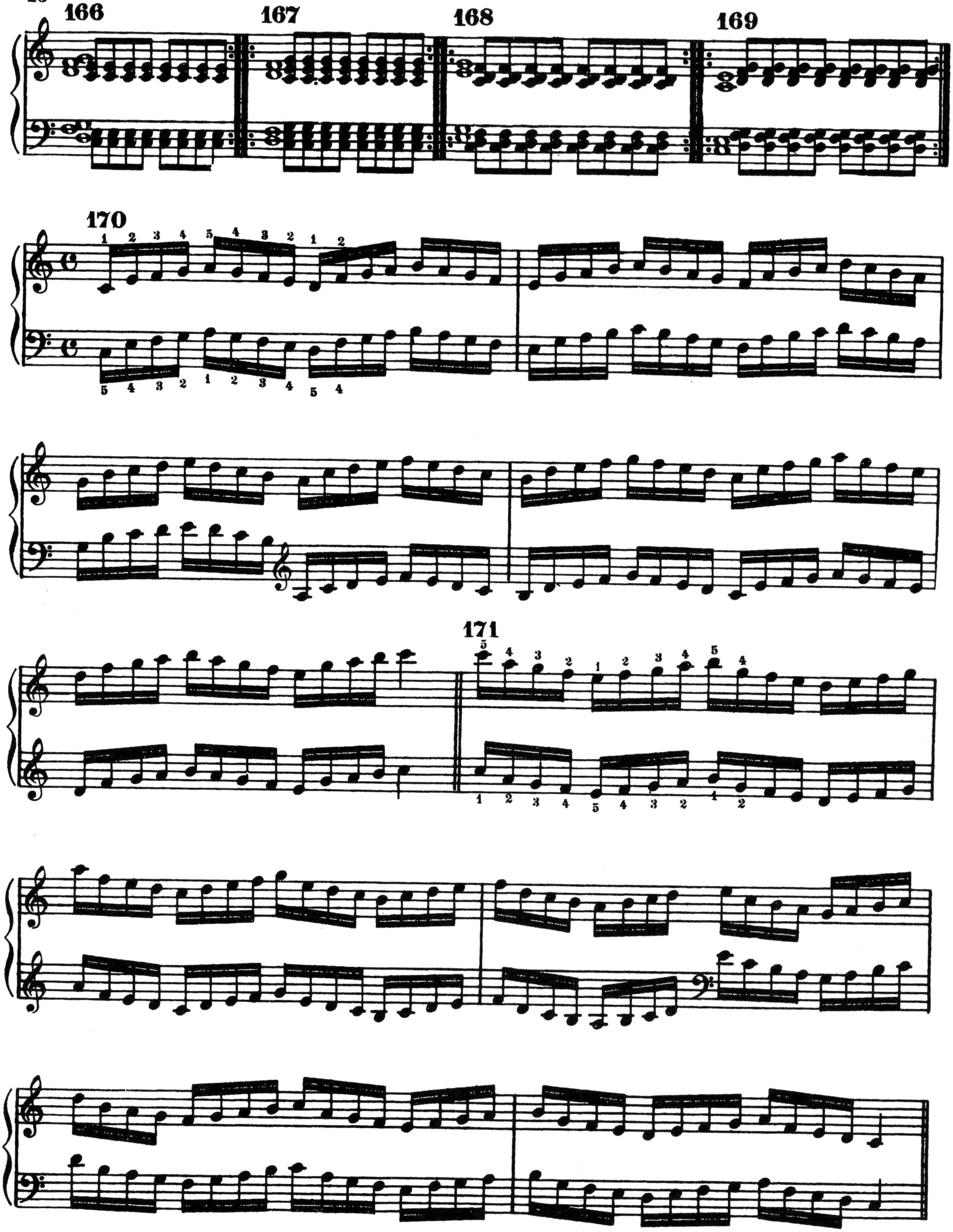
166
167
168
169
170
171

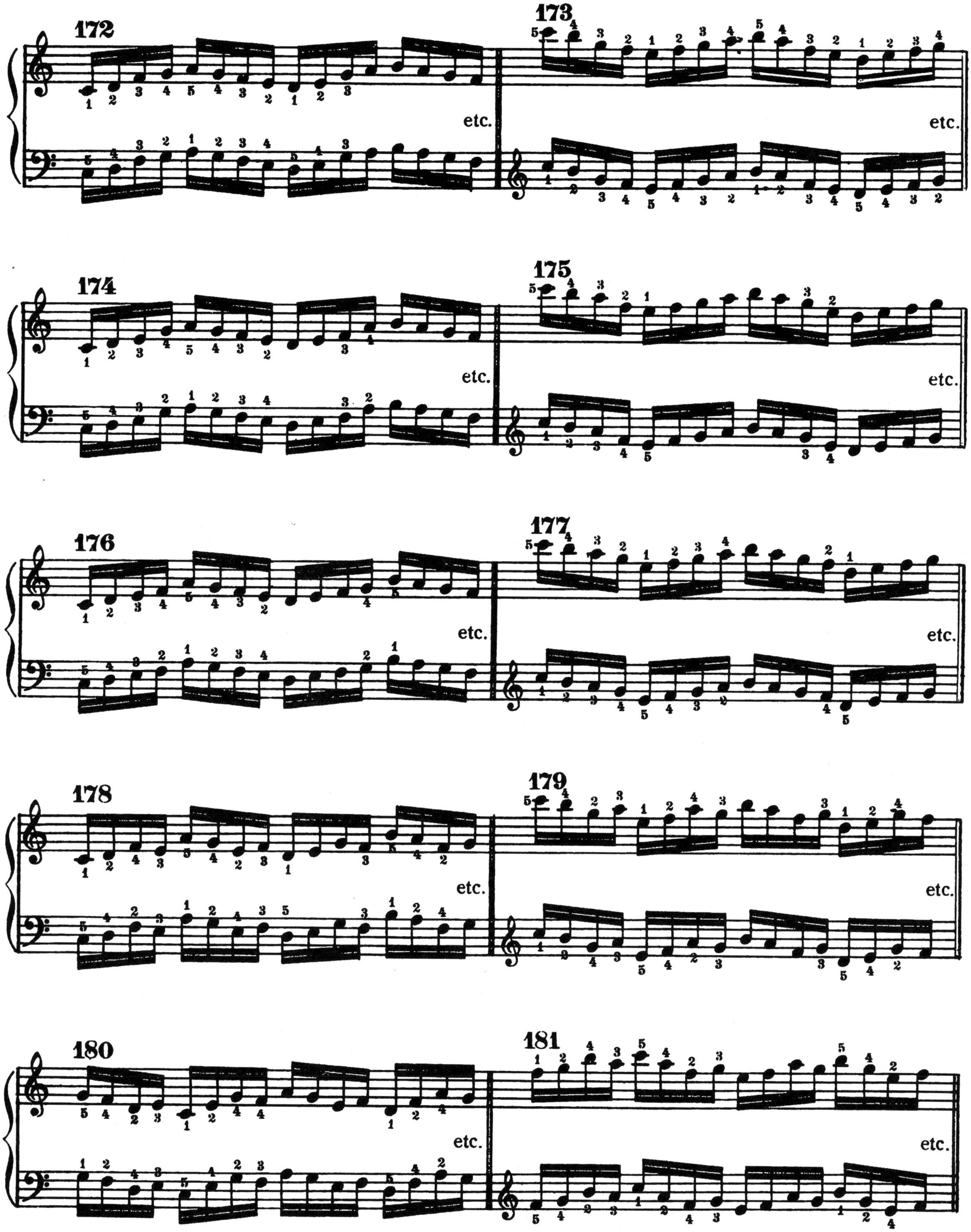
172
etc.
173
etc.
174
etc.
175
etc.
176
etc.
177
etc.
178
etc.
179
etc.
180
etc.
181
etc.

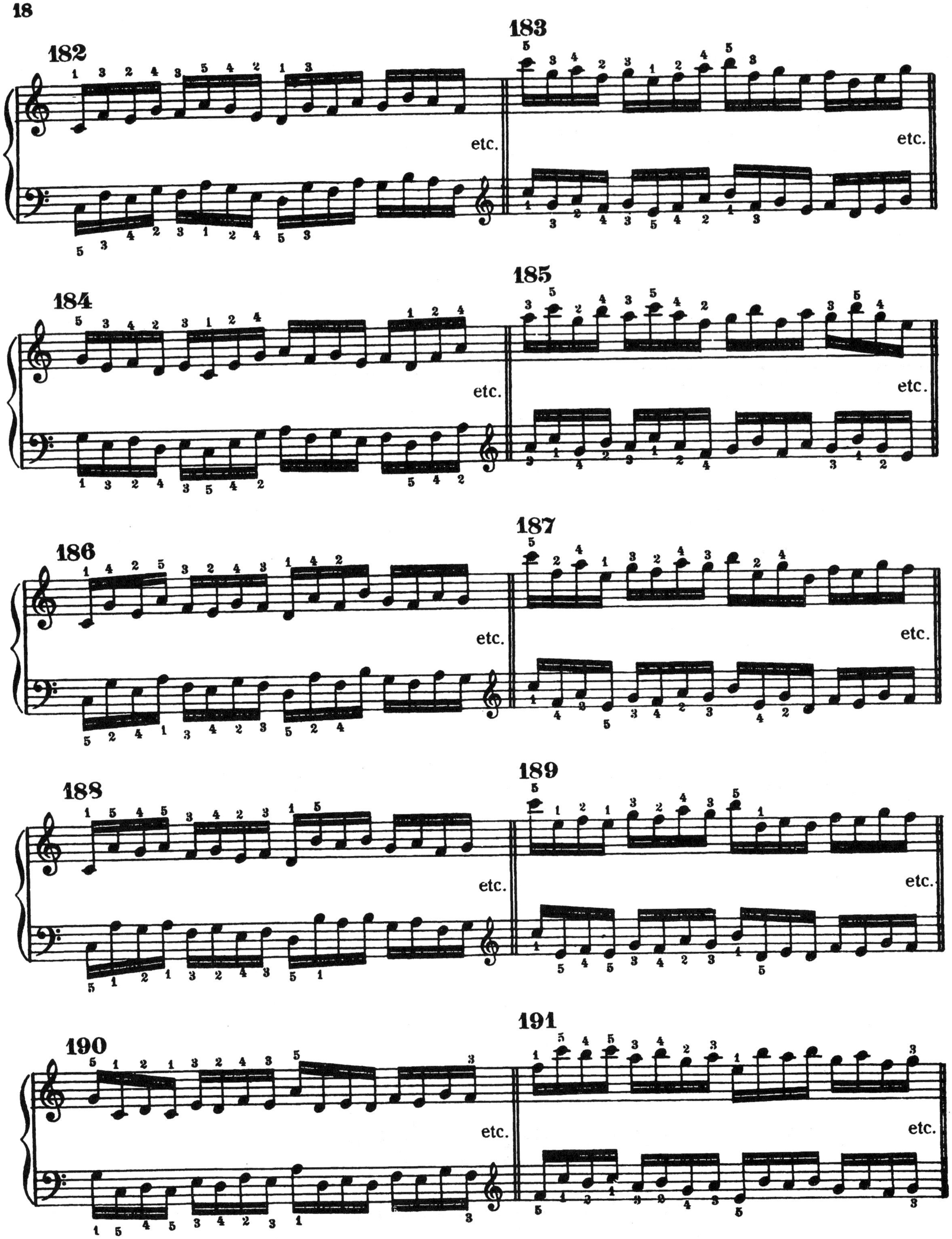
182
183
etc.
etc.
184
185
etc.
etc.
186
187
etc.
etc.
188
189
etc.
etc.
190
191
etc.
etc.

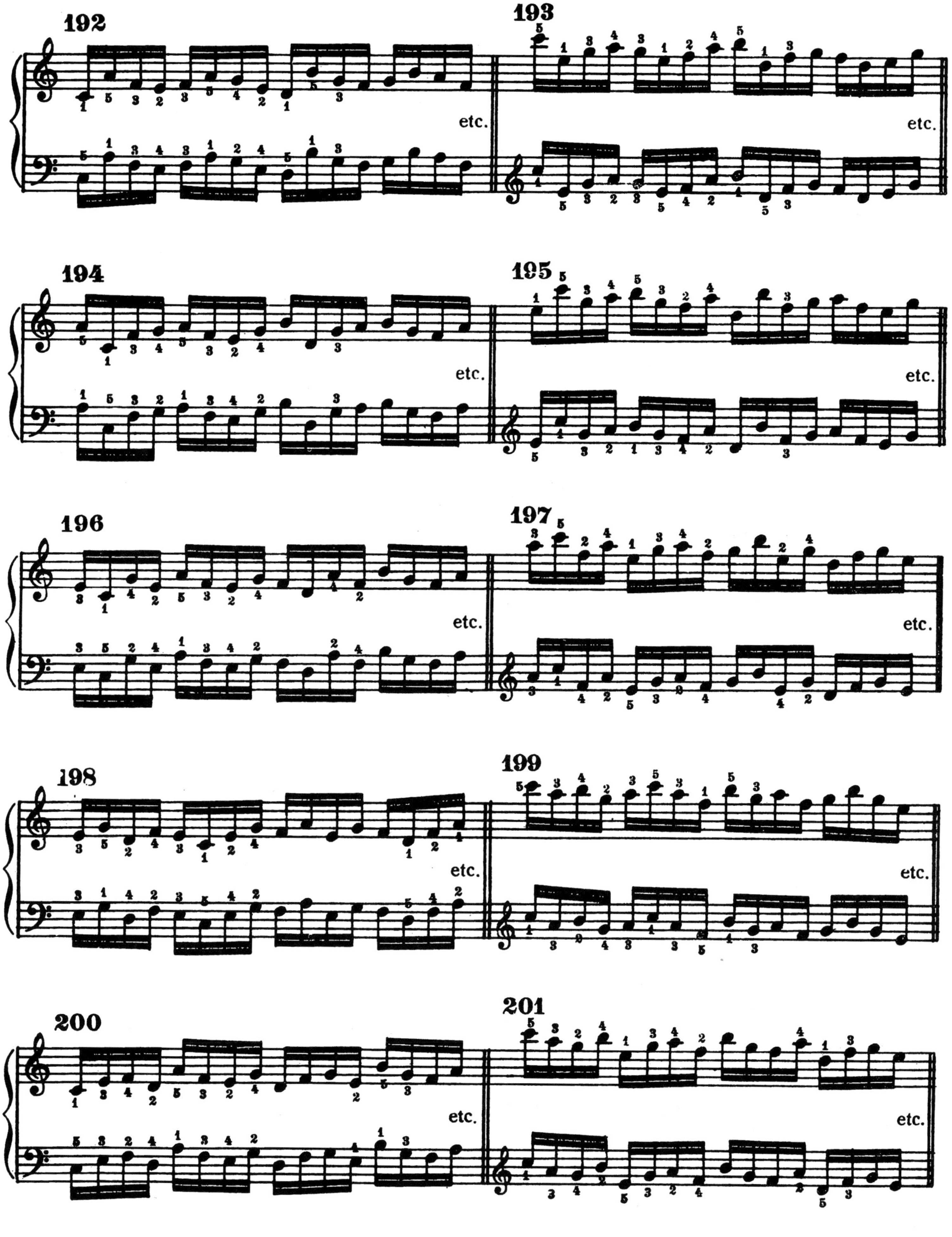
192
193
etc.
etc.
194
195
etc.
etc.
196
197
etc.
etc.
198
199
etc.
etc.
200
201
etc.
etc.

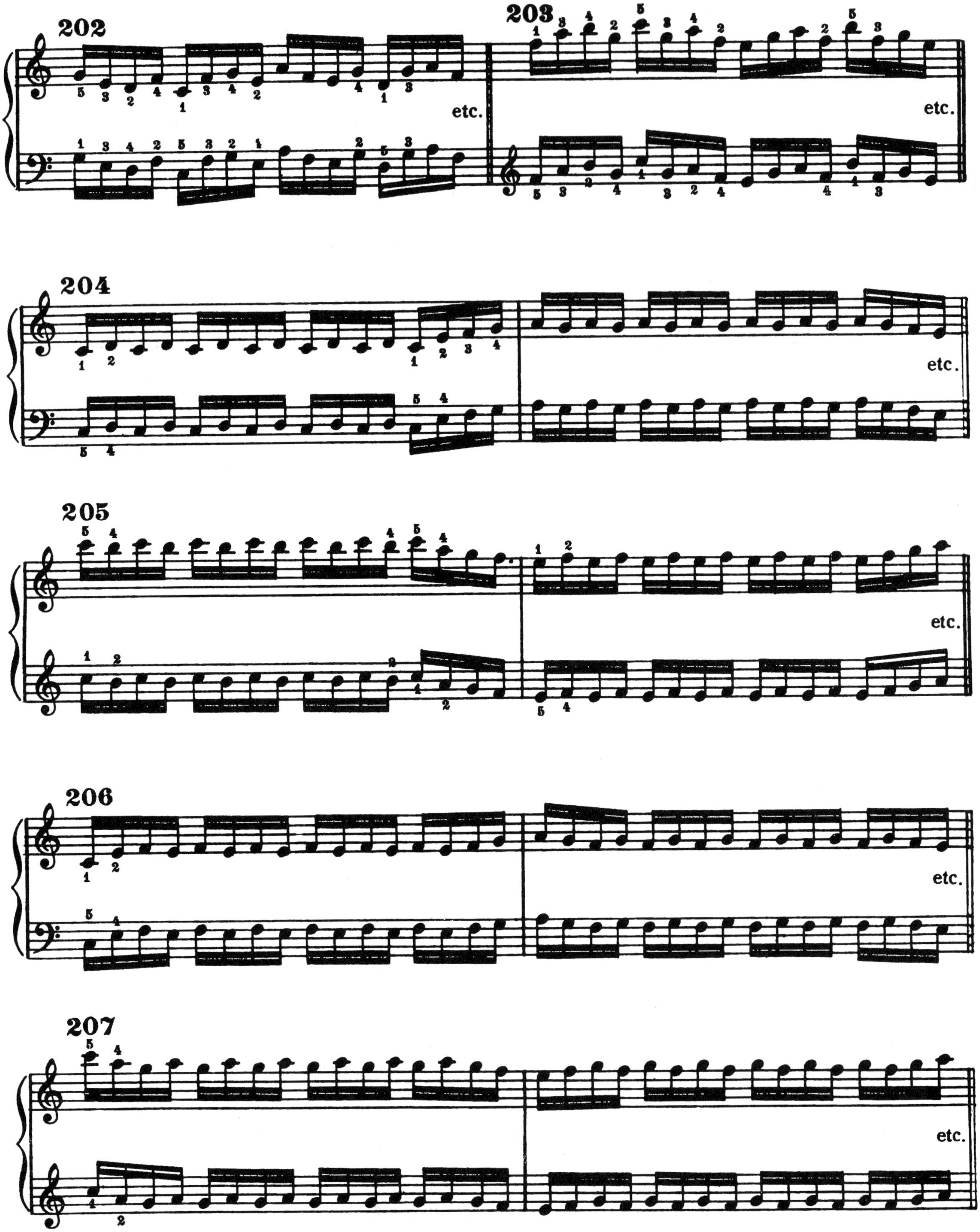
202
etc.
203
etc.
204
etc.
205
etc.
206
etc.
207
etc.

208

209

210

211

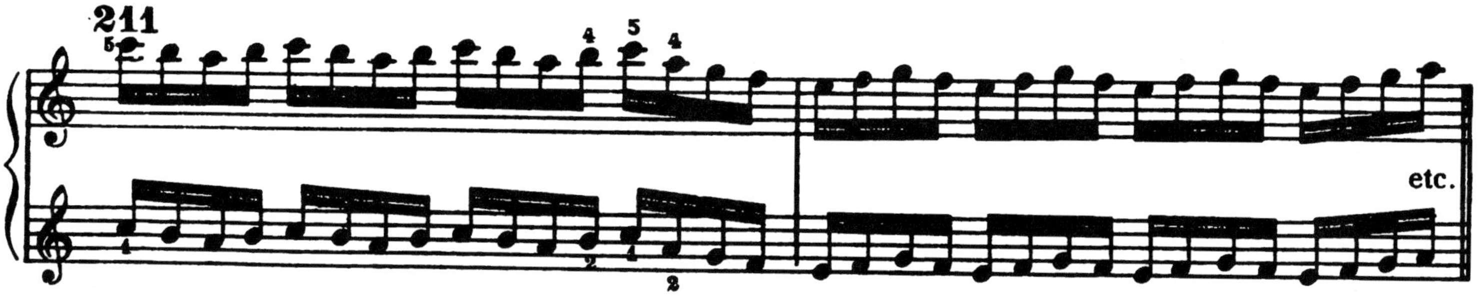

212

213

Preparatory Exercises for Scales and Arpeggios

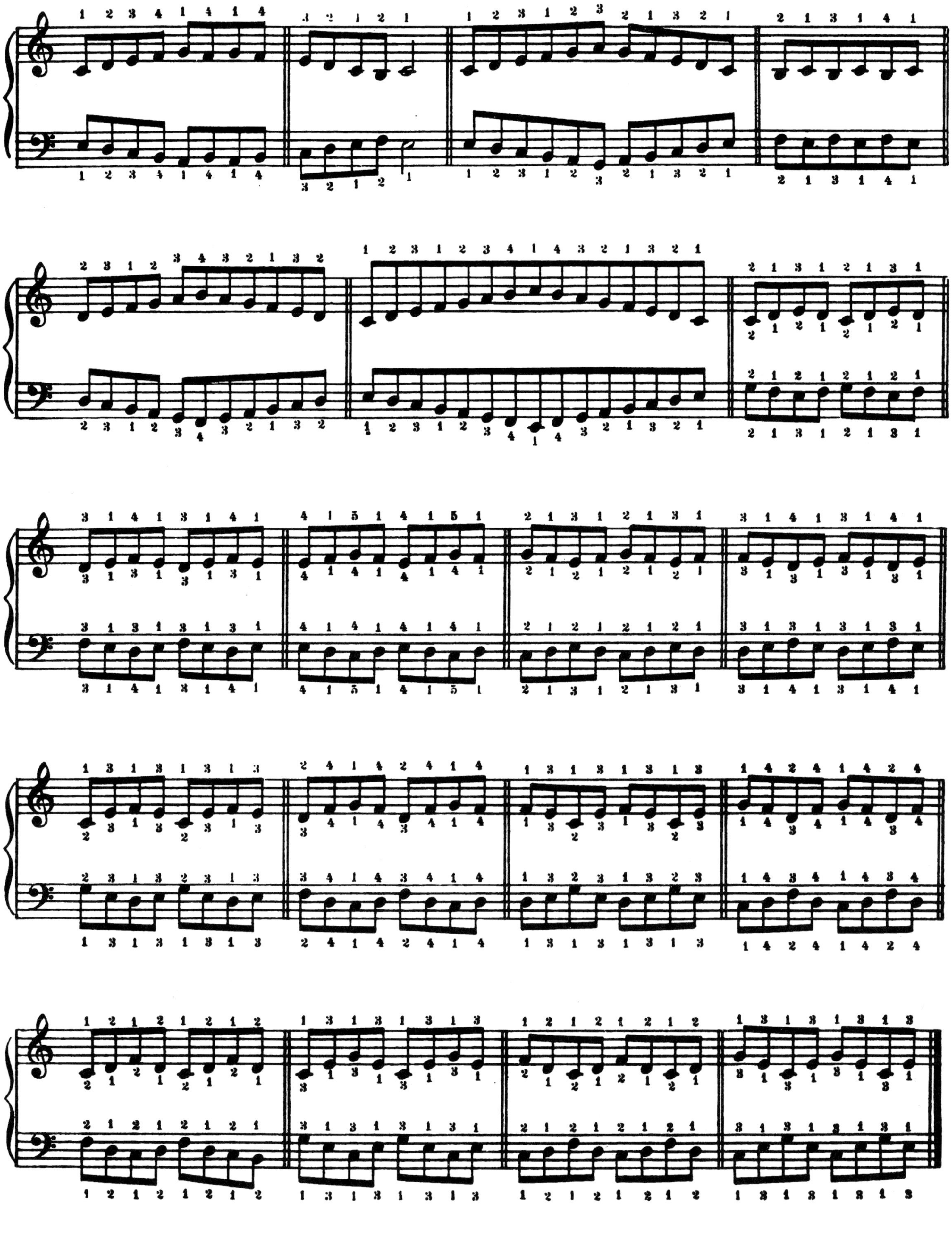

Scales and Chords

in all major and minor keys

by L. KÖHLER

C major–relative to A minor

A minor–relative to C major
(melodic)

A minor–relative to C major
(harmonic)

G major–relative to E minor

E minor–relative to G major
(melodic)

E minor–relative to G major
(harmonic)

Published, MCML, by The Willis Music Co.

D major–relative to B minor

B minor–relative to D major
(melodic)

B minor–relative to D major
(harmonic)

A major–relative to F♯ minor

F sharp minor–relative to A major
(melodic)

F sharp minor–relative to A major
(harmonic)

E major–relative to C♯ minor

C sharp minor–relative to E major

(melodic)

C sharp minor–relative to E major

(harmonic)

B major–relative to G♯ minor

* identical with C flat major

G sharp minor–relative to B major

identical with A flat minor

(melodic)

* Often referred to as *enharmonic equivalents*—alike in pitch, unlike in notation.

G sharp minor–relative to B major
identical with A flat minor
(harmonic)

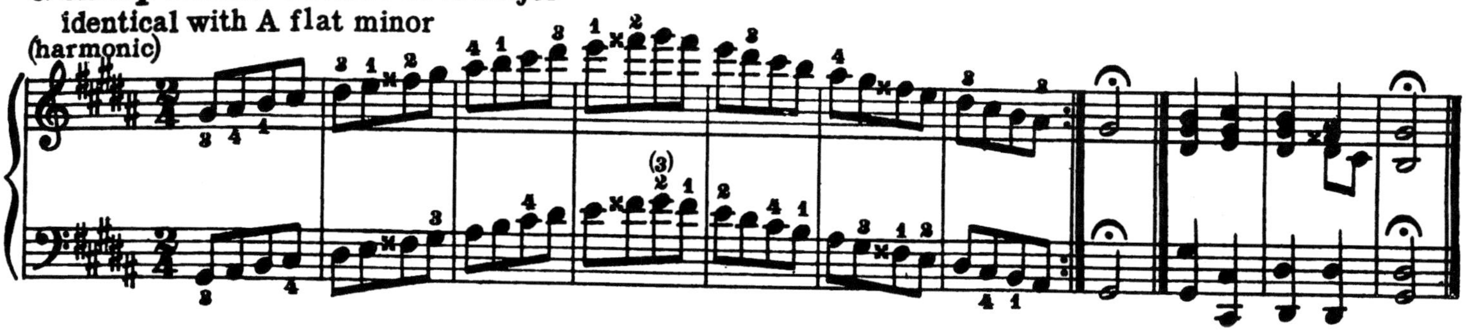

F sharp major–relative to D♯ minor
identical with G flat major

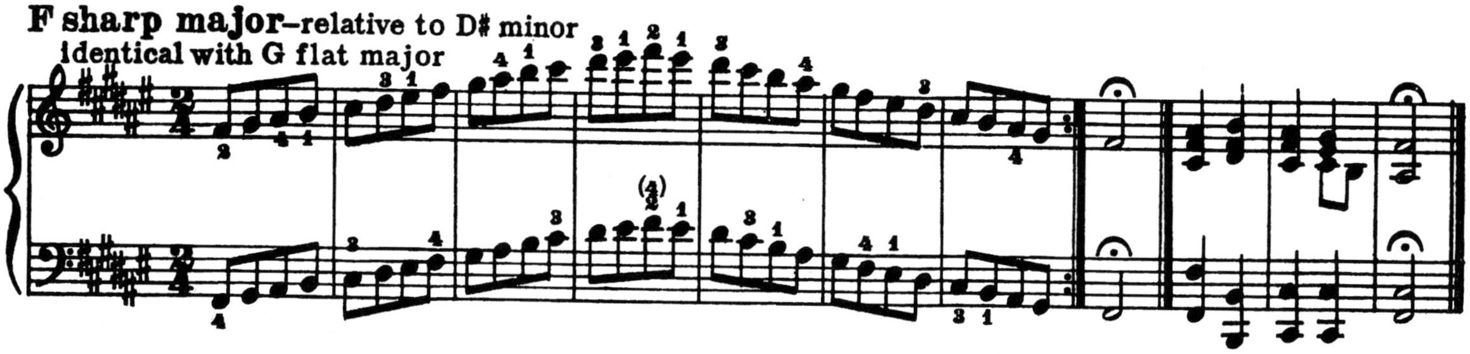

D sharp minor–relative to F♯ major
identical with E flat minor
(melodic)

D sharp minor–relative to F♯ major
identical with E flat minor
(harmonic)

C sharp major–relative to A♯ minor
identical with D flat major

C flat major-relative to A♭ minor
identical with B major

A flat minor-relative to C♭ major
identical with G sharp minor
(melodic)

A flat minor-relative to C♭ major
identical with G sharp minor
(harmonic)

G flat major-relative to E♭ minor
identical with F sharp major

E flat minor-relative to G♭ major
identical with D sharp minor
(melodic)

E flat minor-relative to G♭ major
identical with D sharp minor
(harmonic)

D flat major–relative to B♭ minor
identical with C sharp major

B flat minor–relative to D♭ major
(melodic)

B flat minor relative to D♭ major
(harmonic)

A flat major–relative to F minor

F minor–relative to A♭ major
(melodic)

F minor–relative to A♭ major
(harmonic)

E flat major–relative to C minor

C minor–relative to E♭ major
(melodic)

C minor–relative to E♭ major
(harmonic)

B flat major–relative to G minor

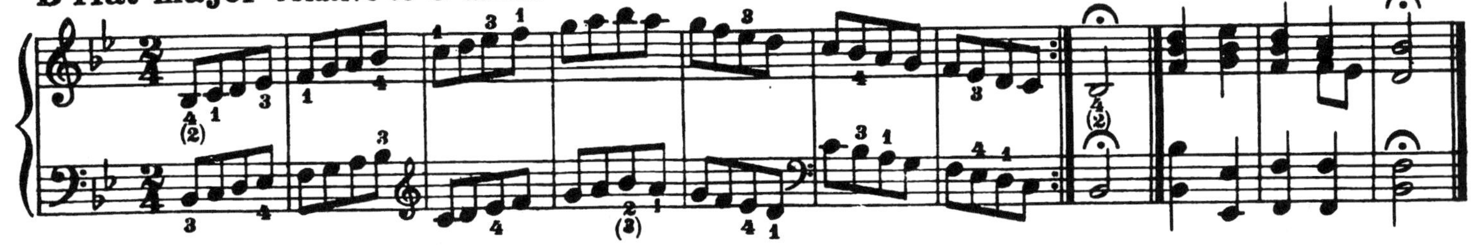

G minor–relative to B♭ major
(melodic)

G minor–relative to B♭ major
(harmonic)

F major–relative to D minor

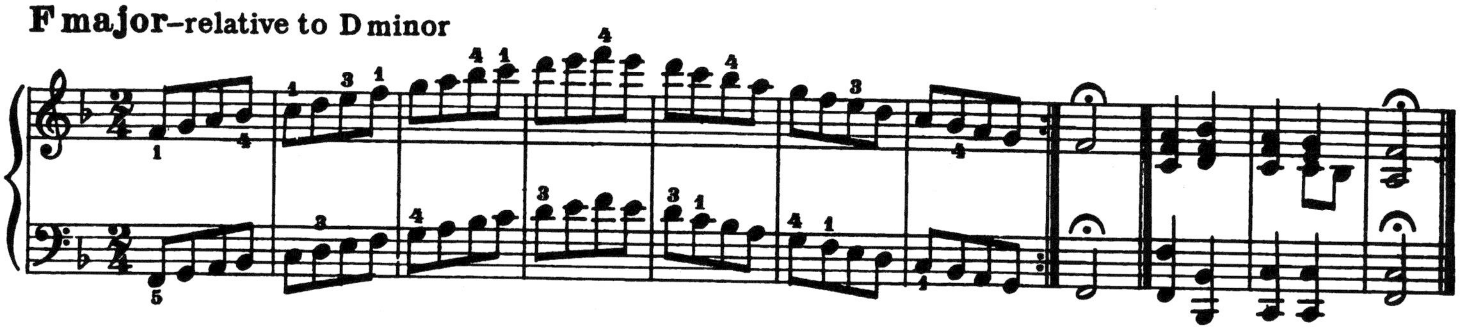

D minor–relative to F major
(melodic)

D minor–relative to F major
(harmonic)

Chromatic scale

Scale, combining the major and minor modes